HEAVENLY
PRAISE &
WORSHIP

Introduction — Psalm 95

Come, let us sing to the Lord and shout with joy to the Rock who saves us. Let us approach him with praise and thanksgiving and sing joyful songs to the Lord.

The Lord is a mighty God, the great king over all the gods. He holds in his hands the depths of the earth and the highest mountains as well. He made the sea; it belongs to him, the dry land, too, for it was formed by his hands.

Come, then, let us bow down and worship...bending the knee before the Lord, our maker. For he is our...and we are his people, the flock he shepherds.

Enter His Presence — Psalm 100

Shout joyfully to the Lord, all you lands. Worship the Great King with gladness; come into his presence with singing. Enter his gates with thanksgiving, and his courts with praise. Give thanks to...bless his holy name. For the Lord is good; his steadfast love endures forever, and his faithfulness to all generations.

The Glory of the Lord — Psalm 8

O Lord my God...may your name be glorified throughout the earth!

When I look at the heavens, the work of your fingers, the moon and the stars that you have established; what are human beings that you are mindful of them, mortals that you care for them?

Yet you have made them a little lower than the angels, and crowned them with glory and honor. You have given them dominion over the works of your hands; you have put all things under their feet, all sheep and oxen, even the beasts of the field, the birds of the air, and the fish of the sea.

O Lord my God...may your name be glorified throughout the earth!

Blessings for the King — Psalm 145

All glory and praise belongs to you, my God and King. Blessed be your name forever and ever. I will meditate on your glorious splendor and celebrate the fame of your abundant goodness. For you...are merciful and mighty, slow to anger and abounding in steadfast love. Your compassion endures throughout all generations.

I will speak of your glory and tell of your power, to make known to all people your mighty deeds, the glorious splendor of your ways. For your kingdom is everlasting and your dominion endures throughout all generations. For you ... are faithful in all your ways and gracious in all your deeds.

By your eternal goodness ... you open your hands to satisfy the desire of every living being. You draw near to those who call upon your name. Open your hands now ... and come to my aid. Pour forth your prosperity into my life; that I may receive the fullness of your abundant blessings.

The Lord's Dwelling Place — Psalm 84

How lovely is your dwelling place, O Lord ... my soul longs and indeed it yearns for the courts of the Lord; my heart and my flesh cry out for joy to the living God. As the sparrow finds a home and the swallow a nest to settle her young, so will I make my home by your altars, O Lord of hosts…my King and my God.

Happy are those who live in your house, ever singing your praise. Happy are those whose strength is in you, whose hearts are set on the path of righteousness. As they go through the valley of the shadow of death they make it a place of springs; the early rain covers it with pools. They go from strength to strength; ever appearing before your presence. O Lord God Almighty…hear my prayer; draw near to me, O God of Jacob!

Better is one day in your courts than a thousand elsewhere. I would rather be a doorkeeper in the house of my God than to live in the tents of wickedness. For the Lord God Almighty in my sun and shield, forever bestowing favor, strength and grace. No good thing do you withhold from those who walk in obedience.

O Lord of hosts…happy is everyone who trusts in you.

Financial Restoration from Job

Blessed are you, O Lord God Almighty, for you are the provider of every abundant blessing. Blessed are you when you give, and blessed are you when you take away.

Blessed are you ... when you laid the foundations for the earth; blessed are you when you established a dwelling place for the light; blessed are you ... when you established boundaries for the sea. O merciful and mighty ... blessed are you when you provide food for the ravens when their young cry out in your holy presence.

O Lord ... you who are surrounded in majesty, radiant with glory, honor and splendor, I call on you now to pour out your abundant blessings in my life. In your eternal goodness, please restore all that evil has stolen from me. Open the floodgates of heaven and bestow upon me the fullness of your enduring prosperity. For you ... can do all things, and no purpose of yours can ever be thwarted.

Ever-Present Provider — Psalm 139

O Lord, you have searched me and you know me. You know when I sit and when I stand; you discern my thoughts from afar. You mark my travels and my rest; and are acquainted with all my ways. Even before a word is on my tongue, O Lord, you know it completely.

You hem me in, behind and before, and rest your hand upon me. Such knowledge is too wonderful for me; it is so high that I cannot attain it. Where can I run from your love? Or where can I hide from your presence? If I ascend to the heavens, you are there; if I make my bed in Sheol, you are there.

If I fly on the wings of dawn and settle beyond the farthest limits of the sea, even there your hand leads me, your right hand holds me fast. If I say, "Surely the darkness shall cover me, and the light of day shall become night," even the darkness is not too dark for you; for the night is as bright as day before you.

For it was you who formed my inward

parts; you knit me together in my mother's womb. I praise you ... for I am fearfully and wonderfully made. Wonderful are all your works, O Great ... my frame was not hidden from you when I was made in the secret place. When I was woven together in the depths of the earth, your eyes beheld my unformed substance.

In your book were written all the days of my life that were formed for me, when none of them yet existed. O Great ... search me and know my heart; test me and know my intentions. Remove any crooked path from me, and lead me in ways everlasting.

A Clean & Pure Heart — Psalm 51

Have mercy on me, O God, according to your steadfast love; according to your abundant mercy blot out my transgressions. Wash me thoroughly from my iniquity, and cleanse me from my sin.

For I know my transgressions, and my sin is ever before me. Against you, you alone, have I sinned, and done what is evil in your sight, so that you are justified in your sentence and blameless when you pass judgment. Indeed, I was born guilty, a sinner when my mother conceived me.

Still, you insist on sincerity of heart; therefore teach me wisdom in my inmost being. Purge me with hyssop, and I shall be clean; wash me, and I shall be whiter than snow. Let me hear joy and gladness; let the bones that have been crushed rejoice. Hide your face from my sins, and blot out all my iniquities.

Create in me a clean heart, O God, and put a new and right spirit within me. Do not cast me from your presence, and do not take your Holy Spirit from me. Restore to me the joy of your salvation, and sustain in me a willing spirit.

Eternal Blessings from Revelation

Holy, holy, holy is the Lord God the Almighty! You alone are worthy to receive glory, honor and power. Great and amazing are all your deeds...just and true are all your ways. For you alone are holy...who was, who is, and who is to come.

I give you thanks...for all nations will come to worship you. O Ancient of Days... clothe me in white so that I will not be put to shame. Restore the passion of my first love...feed me with your hidden manna. Grant me the strength to conquer all forms of darkness, for you alone are worthy to receive glory, honor and power.

Grant me the grace...to obey all your commands; put me through the refiner's fire; help me to accomplish your good and perfect will with patient endurance. Do not blot my name from the book of life, but deliver me from the coming trials that I may receive the crown of life.

For salvation belongs to you, my God...who is seated on the throne; and unto the Lamb...be blessing and honor and glory and might forever and ever!

A Longing for God — Psalm 63

O God, you are my God and for you I long! For you my body yearns; for you my soul thirsts; my flesh cries out for your holy presence as in a dry land without water. As the deer pants for the water brooks, so my soul longs for you, O Great...

For I have looked upon you in the sanctuary, beholding your power and glory. Because your steadfast love is better than life, my lips shall forever praise you. I will bless you as long as I live; I will lift up my hands as I call on your name, O Great...

My soul is satisfied as with a rich feast, and my mouth will praise you as I meditate on you in the watches of the night; for you have been my help, and in the shadow of your wings I sing for joy. My soul clings fast to you for your right hand upholds me. Blessed are you, O Great...

Blessings of Ministry — Psalm 112

Happy are those who fear the Lord, who greatly delight in God's commands. Their descendants shall be mighty in the land, a generation upright and blessed. Wealth and riches shall be in their homes; their prosperity shall endure forever. They shine through the darkness as a light for the upright; they are merciful and obedient.

All goes well for those gracious in lending, who conduct their affairs with justice. They shall never be shaken; the just shall be remembered forever. They shall not fear an ill report; their hearts are steadfast, trusting the Lord. Their hearts are tranquil, without fear, till at last they look down on their foes. Lavishly they give to the poor; their prosperity shall endure forever.

I thank you, O Great...for all your abundant blessings, financial provisions and enduring love. May a mighty torrent of your prosperity flow through my life and into the lives of others, bringing refreshment to a dry and parched land. Open the floodgates of heaven, O Great...as I lay before your throne my life and plans to assist the poor and needy.

The Song of Moses — Exodus 15

The Lord God Almighty is my strength and my salvation. The Lord...is my defense in battle, and I shall exalt in him. This is my God...the God of my forefathers, the God of Abraham, the God of Isaac and the God of Jacob; the great, mighty and awesome God; he is the Rock of my salvation, and to him I turn for protection.

Your right hand, O Lord ... is glorious in power; your right hand, O Lord, has shattered the enemy. When the enemy said, "I will pursue, I will overtake, I will divide the spoil and have my fill," you sent forth your fury. In the greatness of your majesty ... you overthrew the enemy and consumed them like stubble.

I call out to you now, O Lord ... come to my aid. Drive all forms of evil out of my life. Break the chains of darkness that consume me, destroy the demonic influence and shatter the yoke of slavery. Set me free, O Lord ... remove all forms of bondage and oppression from my life, so that I may be purified and consumed by your most holy and loving presence.

Who is like you, O Lord ... among the gods? Who is like you, majestic in holiness, awesome in splendor? In your steadfast love ... you lead the people whom you have redeemed; you guide them by your strength to your holy abode. You bring them into your holy presence, the place where your glory dwells.

Angelic Protection — Psalm 91

You who live in the shelter of the Most High, who abide in the shadow of the Almighty, will say to the Lord, "My refuge and my fortress; my God, in whom I trust." For he will deliver you from the snare of the fowler and from the deadly pestilence; he will cover you with his pinions, and under his wings you will find refuge; his faithfulness will be your shield and rampart.

You will not fear the terror of the night, or the arrow that flies by day, or the pestilence that stalks in darkness, or the destruction that wastes at noonday. A thousand may fall at your side, ten thousand at your right hand, but it will not come near you. You will only look with your eyes and see the punishment of the wicked. Because you have made the Lord your refuge, the Most High your dwelling place, no evil shall befall you, no scourge come near your tent.

For he will command his angels concerning you to guard you in all your ways. On their hands they will bear you up, so that you will not dash your foot against a stone. You will tread on the lion and the cobra, the great lion and the serpent you will trample under foot.

Those who love me, I will deliver; I will protect those who know my name. When they call to me, I will answer them; I will be with them in trouble, I will rescue them and honor them. With long life I will satisfy them, and show them my salvation.

The Lord's Victory — Psalm 118

O give thanks to the Lord, for he is good; his steadfast love endures forever!

Out of my distress I called on the Lord, and the great and awesome...answered me and set me free. With the Lord on my side, I shall not fear; what can mortals do to me? With the Lord on my side, I shall look in triumph on my foes. Better to take refuge in the Lord than to put confidence in mortals. It is better to take refuge in the

Lord...than to put confidence in princes.

All the nations surrounded me; in the name of the Lord I cut them off! I was hard pressed, so that I was falling, but the Lord helped me. The Lord...is my strength and my song; he has become my salvation.

These are the glad tidings of victory in the tents of the righteous, "The Lord's right hand is raised—the Lord's right hand strikes with power. I shall not die, but I shall live, and recount the deeds of the Lord."

Open the gates of victory that I may enter and sing praises to you, O Great... This is the Lord's own gate where the victors enter. I thank you, O Great...that you have answered me and have become my salvation. You are my God, and I will serve you. You are my...and I will worship you.

God's Steadfast Love — Psalm 103

Bless the Lord, O my soul, with all your being bless his holy name. Bless the Lord, O my soul, and do not forget all his benefits. For it is the merciful and compassionate...who forgives all your iniquities, who heals all your diseases, who redeems your life from the pit, who crowns you with steadfast love, who satisfies your every need with his abundant blessings.

The Lord executes righteousness and justice for all those who are oppressed. The Lord is merciful and gracious, slow to anger and abounding in steadfast love. The Great King...does not deal with us according to our sins, nor repay us according to our iniquities. For as the heavens are high above the earth, so great is his steadfast love toward those who fear him; as far as the east is from the west, so far he removes our transgressions from us.

Bless the Lord, all you angels, you mighty ones who do his bidding. Bless the Lord, all you heavenly host, you angelic beings who accomplish his good pleasure. Bless the Lord...all you servants of the Lord, who prosper within his dominion.

The Lord is my Shepherd — Psalm 23

The Lord is my shepherd, I shall not want. He makes me lie down in green pastures; he leads me beside still waters; he restores my soul. He leads me in the paths of righteousness for his name's sake.

Even though I walk through the valley of the shadow of death, I will fear no evil; for you are with me; your rod and your staff, they comfort me.

You prepare a table before me in the presence of my foes; you anoint my head with oil; my cup overflows. Surely goodness and mercy shall follow me all the days of my life, and I shall dwell in the house of the Lord forevermore.

Names, Attributes &
Characteristics of God

Abba Father .... Romans 8:15

Adonai .... Hebrew name for Lord

All Consuming Fire .... Hebrews 12:29

All knowing and infinitely wise .... Omniscient

Alpha and the Omega, the beginning and
the end .... Revelation 21:6

Always present, ever loving .... Omnipresent

Atoning sacrifice for my sin .... 1 John 2:2

Author & Perfecter of my faith ... Hebrews 12:2

Author of life .... Acts 3:15

Blessed Redeemer .... Isaiah 48:17

Bread of Life .... John 6:35

Commander of the angelic army ... Joshua 5:14

Creator of heaven and earth .... Genesis 1:1

Dearly Beloved .... Mark 1:11

El Elyon .... Hebrew name for Most High God

El Shaddai ...... Hebrew name for God Almighty

Emmanuel, God with us .... Matthew 1:23

Faithful and True .... Revelation 19:11

Firstborn of all creation..........Colossians 1:15

For I know my Redeemer lives......Job 19:25

For you are the King of Glory......Psalm 24:7

Fountain of sufficient grace.........................
....2 Corinthians 12:9

Friend of sinners....................Matthew 11:19

Giver of life and everlasting God who in-habits eternity.............................Genesis 2:7

Giver of wisdom, knowledge and under-standing...........................1 Corinthians 12:8

God of my Savior's virgin birth...................
....Luke 1:34–35

God of the poor and stranger......................
....Matthew 25:35–40

Great and amazing are all your deeds..........
....Revelation 15:3

How beautiful you are, my love, how very beautiful........................Song of Solomon 4:1

Inconceivable source of peace and comfort..
....Luke 18:27

Jesus Messiah, my Lord and Savior..............
....Acts 2:36

Just and true are all your ways, O Great King
....Revelation 15:3

Just Judge of the living and the dead...........
....Acts 10:42

King of all kings and Lord of all lords..........
....Revelation 19:16

Lamb of God who takes away the sins of
the world....................................... John 1:29

Life-giving Word in which all things exist....
....John 1:1–4

Light of the World who stepped down into
darkness.. John 8:12

Lord of Glory who was crucified on my
behalf .... 1 Corinthians 2:8

Majestic in glory, awesome in power and
full of splendor .... 2 Peter 1:17

Mediator of the New Covenant in whom
my soul delights........................... Malachi 3:1

Messiah, Son of the Living God ....
.... Matthew 16:16

Most High over all the earth...... Psalm 83:18

My Advocate, the Holy Spirit.......John 14:26

My closest friend..........................John 15:15

My exceedingly great reward...... Isaiah 40:10

My righteousness, sanctification and re-
demption...........................1 Corinthians 1:30

My rock, fortress and deliverer ..... Psalm 18:2

My steadfast love .... Psalm 136:1

Nothing is too hard for you ... Jeremiah 32:17

O God of wonders .... Exodus 15:11

O Great Lover of my soul .... John 3:16

O Great Refiner's Fire who purifies my soul
.... Malachi 3:2

O Mighty One, the profound and incon-
ceivable God .... Luke 1:49

O Righteous One, you are the fullness of
power, glory and victory .... Isaiah 24:16

Precious cornerstone and trustworthy foun-
dation for my faith .... Isaiah 28:16

Precious Living Stone, builder of my spiri-
tual house .... 1 Peter 2:4–5

Provider of every abundant blessing ....
.... 2 Corinthians 9:8

Ransom from heaven .... 1 Timothy 2:6

Refuge for the poor and needy in their
distress .... Isaiah 25:4

Righteous Branch who reigns as King for-
ever .... Jeremiah 23:5

Rock of my salvation .... 1 Corinthians 10:4

Savior for sinners .... Luke 2:11

Send forth your Spirit of love, power and
self-control .... 2 Timothy 1:7

Shepherd and guardian of my soul ....
.... 1 Peter 2:25

Sole Mediator between God and man ....
.... 1 Timothy 2:5

Source and strength for my accomplish-
ments .... Philippians 4:13

Source of eternal salvation for those who
obey .... Hebrews 5:9

Sovereign ruler of all creation......... Acts 4:24

Spirit of God that brings all flesh to life ....
.... Genesis 1:30

Spirit of God who hovers over the deep ......
.... Genesis 1:2

The All Powerful and Almighty.. Omnipotent

The Ancient of Days .... Daniel 7:9

The Bright Morning Star ..... Revelation 22:16

The Chosen One, in whom my soul de-
lights .... Isaiah 42:1

The Glorious One........................ Psalm 76:4

The Good Shepherd who lays down his life...
.... John 10:11

The great High Priest, Jesus Christ, Son of God ....Hebrews 4:14

The Great Physician .... Matthew 9:12

The Lion of the Tribe of Judah who has conquered ....Revelation 5:5

The Lord God Almighty .... Revelation 19:6

The Lord is with me like a dread warrior .....
.... Jeremiah 20:11

The Lord, the God of Abraham, the God of Isaac and the God of Jacob .... Exodus 3:15

The Vine that allows me to bear fruit ....
.... John 15:5

To the King of Ages be honor and glory forever and ever .... 1 Timothy 1:17

Unfathomable giver of all good gifts ....
....Matthew 7:7–11

Victorious and triumphant King.................
....Zechariah 9:9

Who is and who was and who is to come.....
....Revelation 1:8

Wonderful Counselor, Mighty God, Ever-lasting Father, Prince of Peace........Isaiah 9:6

Worthy to receive glory, honor and power...
.... Revelation 4:11

You are always with me .... Matthew 28:20

You are found by those who seek you..........
.... Proverbs 8:17

You are gentle and humble of heart.............
.... Matthew 11:29

You are my rock in whom I take refuge ....
....2 Samuel 22:3

You are my Shepherd, I shall not want ....
....Psalm 23:1

You are near to those with broken hearts.....
.... Psalm 34:18

You are pure, holy and undefiled, majestic
in glorious splendor .... Exodus 15:11

You are the almighty, immortal and invisible
God..1 Timothy 1:17

You are the dispeller of all fear and doubt....
.... Matthew 14:31

You are the image of the invisible God,
firstborn of all creation...........Colossians 1:15

You are the Judge, Ruler and King who
saves us....................................... Isaiah 33:22

You are the Lord, mighty in battle ....
.... Psalm 24:8

You are the Resurrection and the Life ....
....John 11:25

You are the same yesterday, today and for-
ever .... Hebrews 13:8

You are the self-sufficient, self-sustaining God, majestic in power .... Job 37:4–5

You are the Way, and the Truth and the Life ....John 14:6

You are worthy of all my praise ....2 Samuel 22:4

You sustain all things through your powerful word....................................Hebrews 1:3

You will never leave or forsake me ....Hebrews 13:5

You yearn jealously for the spirit that dwells within me ....James 4:5

Your divine nature is understood by all creation .... Romans 1:20

Your plans for my welfare include a prosperous future with hope.............. Jeremiah 29:11

Notes

To allow the reader a unique form of worship, several ellipsis have been inserted into the text. When you come to...take a moment to focus your mind and heart on God. After you enter God's presence, insert any combination of God's names, attributes or characteristics into your prayers. For example, you can replace the word *Lord* with the King of Glory, merciful and mighty Savior, O Great Lover of my soul.

Introduction — Based on Psalm 95:1–7.

Enter His Presence — Based on Psalm 100:1–2 & 4–5.

The Glory of the Lord — Based on Psalm 8:1 & 3–9.

Blessings for the King — Based on Psalm 145:1, 5, 8, 11–13, 16 & 18.

The Lord's Dwelling Place — Based on Psalm 84:1–8, 10–12.

Financial Restoration from Job — Based on Job 1:21, 38:4–41 & 42:2.

Ever-Present Provider — Based on Psalm 139:1–16 & 23–24.

A Clean & Pure Heart — Based on Psalm 51:1–12.

Eternal Blessings from Revelation — Based on Revelation 4:8, 4:11, 15:3, 3:5, 2:4, 2:17, 3:18, 7:10 & 5:13.

A Longing for God — Based on Psalm 63:1-8 & Psalm 42:1.

Blessings of Ministry — Based on Psalm 112:1–9.

The Song of Moses — Based on Exodus 15:2–3, 6–7 & 11–13.

Angelic Protection — Based on Psalm 91:1–16.

The Lord's Victory — Based on Psalm 118:1, 5–11, 13–17, 19–21 & 28.

God's Steadfast Love — Based on Psalm 103:1–6, 8–12 & 20–22.

The Lord is my Shepherd — Based on Psalm 23:1–6.

Back cover text — Based on Psalm 150:1–6.

Cover graphics — Desert Isle Design LLC.

Heavenly Treasure
by Robert Abel

**How well have
you considered your
financial destiny?**

When the stock market
crashes and corporations file
for bankruptcy, the best way
to protect your assets is by
investing in God's kingdom.

In this book, Robert Abel
will help you deepen your
relationship with God based
on a mutual exchange of love. The more we give
to God from a loving heart, the more it blesses
God's heart, motivating him to give back an even
greater return.

The way we live life on earth will determine
our status in the eternal kingdom. By applying the
timeless truths of this book to your life, you will
be able to produce the greatest amount of wealth
for the kingdom of God.

Available at your local bookstore or online at
www.ValentinePublishingHouse.com
ISBN 978-0-9796331-3-3
72 Pages — $5.99 U.S.

Worldwide Adventure
by Robert Abel

Embark on an exciting adventure — the Blessed Trinity has incredible plans for your life!

As the world grows more and more indifferent to spiritual matters, your calling has become even more imperative. Countless souls are depending on you to fulfill your calling in Christ.

In this book, Robert Abel will help you to fulfill your calling in Christ through a simple three-part process: By surrendering your life into the Lord's service, listening to the softly spoken voice of the Holy Spirit and proceeding forth in obedience, you will have the opportunity to embark on the adventure of a lifetime—advancing God's kingdom here on earth.

Available at your local bookstore or online at
www.ValentinePublishingHouse.com
ISBN 978-0-9796331-6-4
72 Pages — $5.99 U.S.

If you would like additional copies of *Heavenly Praise & Worship*, you can order them using the following information. Single copies are free to individuals who write to us. For multiple copies, please use the chart below.

Quantity	Price Each
1	Free
10–25	$ 1.00
35–100	$ 0.80
125–300	$ 0.70
325–600	$ 0.60
750–1200	$ 0.50

Thank you for your generous donation. The above prices include tax and shipping within the United States. For shipments to other countries, please contact us.

Mail your payment to:

Valentine Publishing House
Heavenly Praise & Worship
P.O. Box 27422
Denver, Colorado 80227